RUBANK BOOK OF TRUMPET SOLOS
INTERMEDIATE LEVEL

T0083315

Printable Piano Accompaniments

PLAYBACK+
Speed • Pitch • Balance • Loop

CONTENTS

To access recordings and PDF accompaniments visit:
www.halleonard.com/mylibrary

Enter Code
2431-8516-7615-2817

ISBN 978-1-4950-6507-1

RUBANK®

HAL•LEONARD® CORPORATION
7777 W. BLUEMOUND RD. P.O. BOX 13819 MILWAUKEE, WI 53213

Copyright ©2016 by HAL LEONARD CORPORATION
International Copyright Secured   All Rights Reserved

For all works contained herein:
Unauthorized copying, arranging, adapting, recording, Internet posting, public performance,
or other distribution of the printed music in this publication is an infringement of copyright.
Infringers are liable under the law.

Visit Hal Leonard Online at
www.halleonard.com

Bonita
Valse Brillante

Trumpet

Vander Cook

© Copyright 1943 by Rubank, Inc. (Copyright Renewed)
International Copyright Secured All Rights Reserved

Trumpet

Carnival Of Venice

Trumpet

Air Varie

Henry W. Davis

© Copyright 1942 by Rubank, Inc. (Copyright Renewed)
International Copyright Secured All Rights Reserved

Trupet

Debonnaire

Trumpet

Vander Cook

© Copyright 1943 by Rubank, Inc. (Copyright Renewed)
International Copyright Secured All Rights Reserved

Trumpet

The Cavalier

Trumpet

V. Shelukov
Edited by Wm. Gower

© Copyright 1960 by Rubank, Inc. (Copyright Renewed)
International Copyright Secured All Rights Reserved

Ballade

Trumpet

V. Shelukov
Edited by Wm. Gower

© Copyright 1960 by Rubank, Inc. (Copyright Renewed)
International Copyright Secured All Rights Reserved

Andante

From "Concerto in Eb"

F. J. Haydn
EDITED BY H. Voxman

Trumpet

© Copyright 1962 by Rubank, Inc. (Copyright Renewed)
International Copyright Secured All Rights Reserved

The Executant

Trumpet

R. M. Endresen

© Copyright 1933 by Rubank, Inc. (Copyright Renewed)
International Copyright Secured All Rights Reserved

Fanfare March

Trumpet

V. Shelukov
Edited by Wm. Gower

© Copyright 1960 by Rubank, Inc. (Copyright Renewed)
International Copyright Secured All Rights Reserved

Premier Solo de Concours

Trumpet

Rene Maniet
Edited by H. Voxman

© Copyright 1964 by Rubank, Inc.
International Copyright Secured All Rights Reserved

Punchinello

Trumpet

Vander Cook

© Copyright 1943 by Rubank, Inc. (Copyright Renewed)
International Copyright Secured All Rights Reserved

Trumpet

The Technician

Trumpet

R. M. Endresen

© Copyright 1933 by Rubank, Inc. (Copyright Renewed)
International Copyright Secured All Rights Reserved